Trembling Air

ALSO BY MICHELLE BOISSEAU

East of the Sun and West of the Moon (chapbook)
No Private Life
Understory

Writing Poems (with Robert Wallace)

Trembling Air

Poems by

Michelle Boisseau

THE UNIVERSITY OF ARKANSAS PRESS
FAYETTEVILLE
2003

Copyright © 2003 by Michelle Boisseau

All rights reserved
Manufactured in Canada

07 06 05 04 03   5 4 3 2 1

☉ The paper used in this publication meets the minimum requirements of the American National Standard for Permanence of Paper for Printed Library Materials Z39.48-1984.

Library of Congress Cataloging-in-Publication Data
Boisseau, Michelle, 1955–
  Trembling air : poems / by Michelle Boisseau.
    p. cm.
  ISBN 1-55728-752-X (pbk. : alk. paper)
  I. Title.
  PS3552.O555T74 2003
  811'.54—dc21
                                                2003008339

In memory

F. P. Boisseau 1926–1996

Acknowledgments

I would like to thank the editors of the following journals for first publishing many of the poems in this book:

"Last Weeks of a First Job," "Thorn Gets Theoretical" (as "Thorn"), *Crazyhorse*; "'Envy Has No Holidays,'" "Leaf's Lay of the Everlasting," *Denver Quarterly*; "Visual Dictionary," *Georgia Review*; "Appeal," "Done," "Flood Plain," "Haloes Stippled with Crosses, Roses, Stars and Spears," "Holy House of Nazareth," *Gettysburg Review*; "Another Great Library Burns," *The Journal*; "Relief from Nineveh," *Margie*; "Moon at the Mirror," "Sun Surveys Other Cynosures," *Mid-American Review*; "Luminous Blue Variables," *New Letters*; "Choir of Dust" (as "Dust"), *Ohio Review*; "Lace Sings a Madrigal," *Pleiades*; "Bad News," "The Drop Cloth Drops from the Northern Sky," "Parchment," "Two Winter Pictures," *Poetry*; "American Gothic," *Shenandoah*; "Dog's Ars Poetica," "Talk Radio," *Smartish Pace*; "Briar Rose," "Chronicle of Hammer," "Don't," "The Height of Summer," "Tariff," "Unending," *Southern Review*; "Potato Speculates on Popularity" (as "Potato"), *Tar River Poetry*; "Despair's Rope of Sands" (as "Rope of Sands"), "Constitutional, with My Father" (as "Maj. Payne and Pvt. Joekes"), *Third Coast*; "At My Brother's Place," *Threepenny Review*; "Collect Call," "Steadily," *West Branch*; "Self-Pity's Closet," *Yale Review*.

My thanks also to the University of Missouri Research Board for a grant that enabled me to work on this book.

And thanks to Mark Jarman, Carolyn Kizer, Jeff Greene, Robert Stewart, and especially Tom Stroik, sustenance.

Contents

Acknowledgments *vii*

I.
American Gothic 3
Done 5
Visual Dictionary 7
Briar Rose 9
At My Brother's Place 10
Verge 11
Constitutional, with My Father 13
Self-Pity's Closet 15
Collect Call 16
Tariff 18

II.
Parchment 21
Two Winter Pictures 22
The Drop Cloth Drops from the Northern Sky 25
Holy House of Nazareth 26
Last Weeks of a First Job 28
Haloes Stippled with Crosses, Roses, Stars and Spears 30
Relief from Nineveh 33
Unending 34
The Height of Summer 37

III.
Choir of Dust 41
January's Timetable 43

Chronicle of Hammer   44
Sun Surveys Other Cynosures   45
Moon at the Mirror   46
Thorn Gets Theoretical   47
Despair's Rope of Sands   48
Potato Speculates on Popularity   49
Talk Radio   50
"Envy Has No Holidays"   51
Dog's Ars Poetica   52
Lace Sings a Madrigal   53
Leaf's Lay of the Everlasting   54

IV.
Bad News   57
Another Great Library Burns   58
Appeal   60
Don't   62
Steadily   63
Luminous Blue Variables   64
These Envoys   70
Flood Plain   72

Notes   73

Life is a spell so exquisite that everything con‐
spires to break it.

>   —Dickinson, in a letter

The apple draws the earth as well as the earth
draws the apple.

>   —Newton

American Gothic

A child started to cough and didn't last
the night. Lightning razed the barn.
The gate rotted and livestock trampled
the mustard greens. In the hallways
of rooming houses they waited their turn

for the bathtub. May I put on a light?
Pass the potatoes, please.
When our great-grandparents, the merchants,
posed at their dry-goods counters
in darned stockings and remarkable mustaches,

it hadn't been invented yet. Sure, the sisters
in the kitchen laughed till they cried,
their raw hands clutching at each other,
when the rooster perched on the parlor window
to accompany Aunt Florence in a hymn,

but their smiles floated in the moment,
mild lightning bugs, not lightning
we would learn to aim with camera,
lipstick, and dentistry. In *Collier's*
a tidal wave of hair, coy tilt of the head

and there it was, the Great American Smile
with a Coca-Cola. Before long the President
was walking softly, carrying a big smile.
When you're smiling, let your smile
be your umbrella, chorus lines of teeth relayed

at the Picture Show, the mascot, a cheery mouse
who sang in a tin can. Around classrooms
teachers hung big grins of construction paper:
Dare to Dream. Reach for the Stars.
Roll out the big plans for this town. Big trucks,

big backhoes forging piles of yellow clay
with snappy signage. Our greatness,
began the Senator, our greatness. He
pushed up his sleeves at a stack of pancakes
and launched a grin like a rocket ship

and jets blinked across the sky. Rain fell.
Snow covered the roads and wind worked the fields
where once in a while a farmhouse crouched,
creaking and sighing, thin windows whistling
as someone looked out, provident and hardy.

Done

And then the white gloves fold the flag, falling
snow shut inside, and hand it to my mother-in-law,
good gray coat, fifty-two years married.
Too late now. Where silence ends, it stays.
He never told his children he loved them
or touched them with affection, except a scouring
of the head, or when grown, a handshake,
a tap on the arm. He never apologized.
He couldn't recite Shakespeare, wouldn't stretch out
with an espionage novel or sing in a piano bar
tunes from *Gigi*. He played the accordion
and with his wife at weddings led a polka
expertly among the quick couples, his face
nearly flickering with pleasure. When he read
it was the Stevens Point *Journal*, sales
and obituaries. He learned a trade.
He didn't go to college, or to high school.
Sent off as a farmhand at twelve, he sent money home
that couldn't save the farm. And once in 1935
he watched all night from an open freight car
the billowing immaterial of the Northern Lights.
He didn't spend the war at a desk job,
perfecting pranks on the base's PA system.
He didn't break down, never lost a job.
He measured twice and cut once. He built
a house, he built a bigger house.
He was foreman, he was union.
He never took his children to the circus

and riled the lions with his echoing roar.
He didn't climb the trellis to the porch roof
and wail in the windows at his wife.
He never watched his sons pitch little league,
or appeared in the stands at wrestling matches,
or bragged about them at bus stops.
He was an officer in the St. Joseph Altar Society.
He paid cash for all the weddings
of his daughters he didn't encourage,
and he didn't stagger around the motel pool
in his socks. And in later years if he won
a few hands of pinochle against a visiting son,
he might begin to talk, matter-of-factly,
about Omaha Beach, June 9, 1944,
his company of engineers landing
where the surf was still bobbing, the sand
still festering with burst cartons of bodies,
and over them he lugged his gear, fuel lines
for tanks, fresh grease for the machines.

Visual Dictionary

for my husband and his brothers

April snow that racks against
his well-oiled garage doors
has slicked your faces. Dry them

now, breathe in sweet grease
and metal. Point, shank, head:
here are your father's nails,

here his screws (slotted, Phillips,
Robertson), and a trove
of washers, bolts (hex, toggle,

dead, wing), and nuts ordered
in five-pound coffee cans.
The bandsaw is silent,

likewise the drill. The cold
stove winks and seethes as you
shovel the sawdust in.

The simpler wrenches frown
and smile, and frown and smile
when you turn them around—

they're dumb as hourglasses.
The vise hangs at the end
of its thread, its jaw set:

nothing can speak for him,
not even you, his middle-
aged children. He was hard

to know. And now harder
to lift and hardest to put
back down again is this

maple-handled hammer,
lying where he left it.

Briar Rose

March. Maples waver in their red beginnings.
Buds and violets. Boys in sloppy t-shirts
lope along the railroad tracks, testing their aim
at garage doors. In the thicket behind our house
we tear out briars and hack at honey locust
whose four-inch barbs can pierce a sneaker,

not to mention our daughter running headlong
down the lawn. Stay back, out of the way.
Sinking lopper jaws into a branch, my husband
smirks that in his dominion he won't allow
a slovenly wilderness. Watch out now,
coming through. Thorns biting our gloves,

we hold sprawling bundles at arms-length
like naughty cats, wrestle them, snagging
our jeans, through the trees, and pile them
along the tracks like rolls of barbed wire,
our Maginot Line. Ha! we say, Do not
enter here! To be always vigilant is to sleep

standing up. Such parents doze in doorways
when their pricked daughter swoons. Though a thicket
springs around their heedless girl and ensnares
each errant prince, too soon the briars bloom
and give way, too soon one hundred years,
we wake to see how strangely time has passed.

At My Brother's Place

The TV set whose picture works rides on top
    the TV whose sound does. The stations
    change with a needle-nosed pliers.
From the bed, where he lies most the day,
    draggle sheets flecked with holes
    where his ashes have dropped.
Every surface is covered with the fuzz of ash,
    punctuated by twisted cigarette packs.
His teeth hurt him to wear. From a chair seat
    they grin at a crowd of Coke cans.
Here's the Bible he chants from at night, his third
    this month. They have a way of disappearing
    like the $50 bill I gave him yesterday.

I've brought him salami and cherries. Pumpernickel
    and mustard, a plastic knife to spread it with.
And look, new T-shirts, new socks. A roll of stamps
    and paper, a phone card, an address book
    where I've written all our numbers.
When I've unloaded the packages, and he has eaten
    everything at once, breathing hard, spitting cherry
    pits into his fist,
I walk out to my rental car, clean and empty.

Verge

What kind of end of the world is this
tipped-over weather? A cardinal
is singing the wrong song. The hundred-

year flood came twice in three years. Last week
Boston was baskier than Texas.
Here on the verge of the Great Plains, snow

from yesterday's storm skulks now only
in gullies, thwarted again by the twang
of hearty winds. The hopeful poke their odd

gardens plastered with a pale lettuce
of pansies and daffodils rising
at Christmastime. The rattling grasses

signal in code as the wind snatches
a plastic grocery bag and stuffs it
into a tree's crotch where it sputters

and flaps, a messenger of the new
storm assembling. Even now the winds
of the North are polishing their shafts

and barrels while the ardent forces
of the South make a retreat into
Oklahoma where they'll battle it

out in an ice storm that will lock us
tight and oil the glass roads: Fill the tank,
rent some movies, waddle the firewood

up the back steps, and then batten down
with batteries as the kids raid dinner
rolls and rendezvous under linen

clouds and a wood sky scrawled with crayon.

Constitutional, with My Father

Man and dog shamble past the Photomat
that closed, past the clinic, past Payday Loans,

morning constitutional with vodka
at the finish line. Whatever might pop

into your head to say about this duo—
sad, disgusting, pathetic, or "charming

in a weird way"—you'd be right, this old man
and his little dog, its fur a forest

of soft scabs. If the dog stinks, then the man
stinks to a higher heaven. Behind him he drags

the lop-eared dog by an ancient belt looped
around its neck, *her* neck, a little bitch.

She lopes along behind him proudly, tongue
dropping starbursts of drool on the sidewalk.

If he left her all day in the hot sun
tied to a bus stop sign, she wouldn't feel it

a disaster, and when he stumbled back,
she'd still thrash her tail, paw his grimy pants

and lap the water he'd hold in his hands.
I can speak with some authority here.

With scissors borrowed from the ICU
(no-you-don't) nurse, I clipped—rather, I sawed—

the long yellow toenails curled like frozen
comets over my father's toes. Eight IVs

dangled like udders around his bed
as four monitors gave weather reports

from his planet, and one ventilator,
(labeled "Amadeus") shook him each time

it bellowed oxygen into his lungs.
Not the first time he couldn't feel a thing,

not the last, not yet. His toenails were jagged
and crusted with God-knows, but I kept plying

the scissors at them. His feet were so cold
my hands stung, but I kept at my small job

because what's worse than a droll dog dancing
on the end of a belt is the dog loose

and dragging her leash behind her down the road.

Self-Pity's Closet

Appetite without hunger, unquenchable
thirst, secret open wounds, long parades
of punishments, anger honed and glinting
in the sun, an empty bird call, the wind
driving a few leaves, the grass bent down,
shivering, running in place, far off a dog
barking and barking, the skin sticky, the crotch
itchy, the tongue stinging, words thrust from the mouth
like bottles off a bridge, tangy acids
of disgust, dank memory of backs, of eyebrows
raised, cool expressions after vast and painful
declarations, subtle humiliations creeping up
like the smell of wet upholstery, dial tone
in the brain, days swollen and matted
like newspaper melting in the bathtub,
the conviction your friends never really
loved you, the certitude you deserved
no better, never have, the faucet drilling
the sink, a bug bouncing against the window:
go away, make them all go away.

Collect Call

Whatever he means, my brother means no harm.
It's 6 A.M. in his time zone. Was he awake
all night dreaming up these children? A girl
my daughter's age named Music
and twelve-year-old twin sons
born six months apart:
Seth Gábriel and Seth Gäbriel, named
for an archangel of double messages
whose secret translations my brother keeps.

And he meant no harm years ago
when he scooped up a toddler at the zoo
and ran with her as far as Monkey Island
before the crowd pried away the child he fought
to save from them. While he was strapped
onto the stretcher and lifted, a cracker on a plate,
he watched me watch him speed away,
climb the stairs that wind through a hole
in the clouds and close around him like an eye.

"Oh, I have lots of children,"
he suddenly remembers, "lots and lots,
but I never get to see them."
Perhaps each tooth he lost was sown
into a child that sprang up like a god
with a fanciful name. I hunch the phone
against my shoulder and try not to set him off:
"And how do you manage to support them all?"
"I give them lots of ideas."

Upstairs I hear doors slamming, the kids
awake, running, laughing, a game
of can't-catch-me. The winner chooses
the place at the table; the other pours the milk.
But couldn't he have real children? A woman
somewhere could have slowly undressed
this small nervous man and given
him proof he wasn't denied
every fruit in the garden—children,
jobs, houses, beds—our easy windfall.

Tariff

It takes time to appreciate how I once
made a friend so unhappy the next night
on the road from Chauncey to Amesville, Ohio,
she steered her Fiat Spider head on
into an on-coming truck. Her boyfriend
identified her waitress uniform.
She's been dead now for more than twenty years.
What I did to hurt her I won't tell you—
so you're free to imagine any vicious,
self-indulgent, hapless blunder or crime

while I go about turning this into a poem again,
turning over heavy marl, the garden
in spring, and the wind picks up, flinging soil
against my neck, behind my ears, into my teeth.
You have to get dirty: what *appreciate*
means is *to price*. After living a while
you understand the ways you have to pay.

Parchment

I'm holding in my hand the skin of a calf
that lived six hundred years ago, translucent
skin that someone stretched on four strong poles,
skin someone scraped with a moon-shaped blade.
Here is the flesh side, it understood true dark.
Here is the hair side that met the day's weather,
the long-ago rain. It is all inscribed
with the dark brown ink of prayer

(the acid galls of ancient oaks), though these reds
(deluxe rivulets that brighten the margins)
are cinnabar ground to a paste; another paste
of lapis lazuli for these medieval skies;
and for flowering meadows or a lady's long braids
the yellow arsenic *orpiment*
whose grinding felled the illuminator's
boy assistants like flies, or like kermes, insects

whose pregnant bodies gave pigment; and the goose
who supplied quills, the horse its hair, and flax
the fine strong thread that held the folded skins
into a private book stamped with gold for a king.

Two Winter Pictures

Très Riches Heures of Jean, Duke of Berry

1. January: A Very Fine Time, Indeed

Inside the rare book, a painting, in the painting
    a tapestry of knights crashing and falling
        in a cascade of helmets. It hangs in the banquet hall
where homely Duc de Berry among his retinue and gold plates

welcomes guests from the cold: *approche approche* he says
    in gold-leaf. Hands stretched toward their patron or toward
        the fire they painted behind him, the Limbourg
brothers enter their masterpiece with their wives. In crafty gags

we can only guess at, the brothers set before us
a scene that translates *Noblesse oblige* as *Be generous*
    to artists. Small feathery dogs stroll companionably
        among platters of woodcock on the damasked table.

A knightly drinker is dwarfed by the gold bowl he drains
and the duke eclipsed by the glowing brocade
    only the rich could wear. Somehow the cocky courtiers
        deeply slighted the painters: from cup bearer (wearing one spur!)

and carver, the hilts of their daggers jut out just so—
pizzles prompted for coupling, but no likely place disposed.

2. FEBRUARY: CRYING WITH A LOAF OF BREAD IN YOUR HANDS

Leaving the shelter in January's
    lush illumination,
we come to skim-milk snow,
        pewter sky, seedy rations

pigeons pick from farmyard droppings.
    But through beehive and kindling
in bundles, sheepcote and a donkey
        driven to a distant village,

the painting shows peasant life
    that might content a duke.
Through cut-away walls of the quaint
        cottage he could look

at clothes hung to dry by a modest fire
    that warms three figures.
One is a woman in a blue dress
        that she lifts demurely

to her knees. Behind her are men—
    we see when we look close—
for they've hitched their wet tunics
        above their thighs to expose

dangling genitals. A lampoon for—or on—
    a childless patron? Or on her?
But she's learned to ignore the antics
        of her husband's celibate (since poor

and landless) younger brothers. Farmhands
      on the farm that's never theirs,
they fling seed, flail grain, gather fruit
      and never hope to marry;

even a rude encounter in town
      takes hard cash. End of the road
for their genes' long lines
      fizzling in the dangling stones

they tease her with, in that damp house
      on a long-ago day
imagined with fresh paint by living men
      while the matter of our own making

coiled in thousands of nameless strangers
      with the dumb luck to escape
siege, plague, prison, famine, and fire
      just long enough to mate

with another sturdy soul, giving
      us the length of our bones, the black
in our hair, a weakness for salt
      and this strange run of luck.

The Drop Cloth Drops
from the Northern Sky

The radio reports four inches of snow
has astonished Paris and delivers
a spectacle of stuck trucks, baffled roads,

and commuters spending the night in their cars.
How the mess must annoy the exacting
French, inventors of bureaus and guillotines,

diplomacy and brassieres. Snow belongs
on ski slopes not among the temperate.
But there it is, coming down, blunter

of edges, great leveler. It obscures
the great on their pedestals and uniforms
the dumpster in a fountain of cream.

Holy House of Nazareth

Francisco de Zurbarán, oil on canvas: 1635–1640

The weather in the window above Mary
threatens rain, though across the room the window
above young Christ lets down a sunbeam stair.
It seems the son of God has pricked a finger

and in bemusement holds the drop of blood
into the light to get a better look.
His mother from her gray place isn't blind
to the little twist. She's angry and sick

of how casually he wears pain, a boy
who appears all of fifteen, chestnut curls,
daredevil, the kind you see on skateboards
blitzing past, and later watch pulled from cars.

She won't open her mouth. Why waste her breath?
She's turned her head to hide the ready tears:
why in the first place was he messing with
those thorns? Two sticks have spilled on to the floor,

others tangle in his lap. Was he breaking off
the thorns to make some kind of tool? Or nails?
On her none of this irony is lost.
She wears a thimble, but I see no needle.

The sunlight pours on him relentlessly.
Something's odd there. I stand up, cross the room:
bobbing in the sunbeam are amoretti,
fatuous pudgy cherubs in a troupe:

divine love swarms above the chosen boy
as shadows play with her who has no choice.

Last Weeks of a First Job

My students' carefully calibrated
boredom seeped over their Italian boots
and oozed up the aisles toward me at the lectern
who sidestepped it, reading from the fat text:
So farewell Hope, and with Hope farewell Fear,
Farewell Remorse: all good to me is lost;
Evil be thou my Good. "Notice the vigor,"
I started saying, "of his rationale,
the rolling r's, the spitting fricatives . . ."
Their faces only drooped the more. For them
to cross the plains of Milton was too addling,
too arid—the old blind poet was tormenting
the young again, language that drummed and clanged
about a sexy damnation and damned
dull sex. Out the window behind their backs,
10 miles away, Mt. Holston and I traded
a look. It was blue where afternoon creased
its ravines, green where trees were leafing out
while I—dark intensity at the blackboard—
was reading about a wall, *a circling row*
Of goodliest trees loaden with fairest fruit,
Blossoms and fruits at once of golden hue. . . .
At the foot of the college hill, a truck
was shifting into low gear to start the climb
and pushed its roar before it like a broom.
A pilot light flickered in my students' eyes,
their bodies unslumped: finally a real contest,
a struggle over noise they understood.

One Gate there only was, and that look'd East,
my voice climbed word by word against the truck
coming on, grinding, down-shifting, wave shaking
the windows as I read, *and in contempt,*
At one slight bound high overleap'd all bound
Of Hill or highest Wall, and sheer within
Lights on his feet. As I crooned the last notes,
the dispirited truck expired in a cough.
My eyes burned and swept the awakened room.
"That's the way," I said to the blue beyond
their raised heads, "evil enters paradise."

Haloes Stippled with Crosses, Roses, Stars and Spears

I'm in heaven and in Kansas City,
alone except for the guard looking in,
inattentive and tired. Latin rides

furling ribbons. Crushed lapis
robes the disembodied
who dwell in metal air. Gold skies

fill my eyes. Books fill my head.
About, about. A siege stratagem
required flinging the plague dead

over the defending walls. The besieged
could hope for dew to lap from roofs,
bread thinned with sawdust, and work

in Siena continuing on this altarpiece
which declares painter and his grubby
assistants are in love with God

as I used to be. Reverent, rosaried,
I was a singer of hymns to Mary and May.
The chords are still so tangled in me

that standing in this overheated museum
I can call them up, and with them
flowers carried to school in jelly jars

for the classroom altar. Through Spelling
and Arithmetic the low notes of roses
drowned the smell of chalkdust, baloney

in lunch boxes, and us. Was I just
a lover of my body's pleasure?
of redolence, pretty music and pictures

like these gawky blond angels
with rainbow wings? My eyes brim,
my head swims with books and books

and eyes contend over the field of beauty.
The beauty of surfaces, the beauty
of truth. The shame. Gold beat

into monstrances and sword hilts,
gold that bought and squandered armies
came from Africa. These haloes, these lyres,

this paradise might have been scooped
from a spangled river Europeans didn't know yet,
the Tinkisso, Joliba, Falémé,

then traded with Berbers who trod
the secret routes back to Sijilmasa.
Trade comes from *tread*, from thousands

of feet making a path: Not me, I didn't start it,
I was only following the way.
Along with gold in the caravans

another rarity: slaves from Guinea, prized
from China to Portugal. Prince Henry's
lateen-rigged caravel nosed along

the African coast looking for gold,
for a way around the Muslims and returned
with human plunder. It was written

some were meant to serve, but that's a soft
translation: *servus* means *slave*. And better,
said the popes, to be slave to a Christian

than free to worship heathen gods.
Constantinople had fallen and the trade
meant labor for the sugar islands,

gold for wars against the infidels
and for the glory of God who might have heard
the crying from his golden throne.

Relief from Nineveh

After a glance outside at sunlight crashing
through clouds and thinning trees—I turn back here
and find an Assyrian has entered
my poem. He strokes his chain-link beard

and one-eyes me like a jack of hearts.
From his hand a lotus stem curls, a monstrous joke
of a phallus. He's my favorite figment
when I have fears, my totem of hope

against the large darkness the stars
have never broken. This laughable bit
of life, our sip from the ancient indifferent
fountain inflicts him too. Why not worship

the sun and big-bellied women? and accept
that wisdom is the province of the lord
of the deep, the underplace we're heading for
"where dust is the fare and clay the food."

Unending

We went to trouble ourselves in a place
of heavy occasion. It was a wet March dawn.
Sleet stuck pins to our coats as we scaled
the subway stairs to former East Berlin,
then got lost among new Mercedes showrooms
and buildings blasted out for fifty years: the fall
of communism as the spring of capitalism.
Our hotel eyed a domed church humbled
by construction cranes. They hung over it
like checkmarks, a child hunched beneath a board
that chalks up his infractions.

At the Institute, an ice storm of resentment
broke between old East and old West Berliners,
and my husband spilled his research
in a rush of English that rankled them the more.
Then came the luncheon. *Hackenpeter
vom Schwein* or *Schlactplat?* Both
were stiff mounds under tarps of gravy.

◆

A cold mist filled the air but didn't fall.
I managed to pry off a raisin-sized bit
of the Wall though it was fenced against vandals.
Beside it, in former free Berlin, the ruins
of Gestapo Headquarters. A place
of heavy occasion getting heavier.
That's the way it goes, straw upon straw.

To say I can't bear anymore, we've walked days,
the children are shaking with hunger,
means the machine guns come out, means
there's blood in the baby's stool.
Then your shoes get stolen.

When my friend Achille was a boy in Italy,
he didn't cry when the fascists marched
into the square a pregnant villager
and shot her for letting a partisan
steal a chicken. He didn't cry
when the retreating army blew up the station
and limbs and bits of button rained and drizzled.

It was the cart-horse that made him cry.
Tail shooing off flies, it had been waiting in harness
to be tapped with a whip when the explosion
lifted it up and smashed it like an apple
against the bricks of the telegraph office.

And there it hung for all to see.
Though bodies and parts of bodies
littered the station yard, and those still alive
moaned *(for the love of God help me)*,
the people pointed at that dead animal—
that took no sides, that wanted only grass—
and they cried. And forty years later
Achille's tears slipped loose as he told me.

And so it was not the ruined detention cells
where the Gestapo dumped prisoners

after interrogation. It wasn't descending
to the makeshift museum in the cellar kitchens,
nor the photographs of face after face
of those who entered there. But one face.

The word "Wisconsin" jumped out.
My husband's home state, dairy farms, broad minds,
Poles, Germans, and good government.
The caption: *Mildred Harnack-Fish (1902–1943)
in 1942 while in Gestapo detention,*
a UW lit prof who'd married
a founder of Red Orchestra, the resistance group.

She was looking calmly at her Nazi photographer.
She'd pulled her dark hair back tight,
as I do when about to start a job, and appeared
yet unhurt though I read she was tortured
and the next winter executed. Around me
old bricks, display cases, some school kids
reading about the burning of the synagogue.

Under glass the open volume of Goethe
she had with her when arrested. A priest
who visited her had saved it. In the margin,
in a grave dark hand, her translation reads:
*All is given by the Gods, the unending Ones,
To those whom They love—They withhold nothing,
All joys, unendingly,
All pain, unendingly, They withhold nothing.*

The Height of Summer

> *Old death is so beautiful—so very beautiful—We will die together—I know—*
> —Zelda Sayre, letter to Scott Fitzgerald, 1919

The secret to picking blackberries is eating
them at once. Bike in the grass, poison ivy
lapping your knees, plunge your hand in
after the sweetest, shiniest multiples—

time is won only in the lust of now.
The lovers are drunk in bed at the Plaza.
Luscious daughter of an Alabama judge,
charmed young writer from snowy Minnesota,

their quick bodies shine with the unguent
of urgent love. I want to praise their callow
confidence in the future, praise the ooze

of headlong minutes that sweeten the taste
of berries and the dark juice suspended
with the seeds of what becomes of us.

Choir of Dust

I am small, I am smoke,
                    vapor you can
taste. Ocean suds rolling on a beach in
Argentina
            hold me, and I hold all
seas, leaf-meal and pollen, rhino powder,
star parts, cinders from Jeanne
                        d'Arc's pyre, crushed dry-
wall, dander sloughed off in your first coupling,
a Nabokov
            butterfly's scales, a bit
of Whitman's bootsole, a bit of his beard.

(I am small, I contain
                    multitudes.) I
am the library of Alexandria
and popsicle
              sticks, Ankor Wat's temples
and dandelions, the quiet workshops
of Dresden, the loud work-
                  shops of Detroit,
Donne's St. Paul and Irene Dunne's nail polish,
the True Cross and
                crumbled crosswalks. Midge, mite,

inconsiderable quark, infinitely
trivial; that is, every-
              where. Cosmic joke,

monumental truth, universal prayer,
of endings, big
                    cliché, prosaic snow.
Voice of the future, voice of the past, voice
of the present falling
                    through the trembling
air. I am we, and we are it, softening

the furniture,
            floating onto window-
sills and into your shoes that stand at your
bed as if another
                    you watched over
the sleeping you, drifting, drifting onto
your sleeping face.

January's Timetable

    I'm my own kind
of comfort, the bare facts,
    iron and lead.
Loud August with its sex,
    gauzy April,
sighing the day long, spout
    philosophies
of confusion, runoff
    and mud, dust swirl,
pollen, grainy pictures.
    I'm fair and square
and literal like the law:
    the secret heart
is no creamy center.
    La, la, go sing
about snow-crusted buds,
    how spring's coming.
But not toward you. Beat your
    arms, stomp your feet
on the icy platform
    as signs creak while
you look up and down
    the tracks. The two-
faced clock faces both ways
    of now and no
trains come. See how I smile
    and I'm all teeth.

Chronicle of Hammer

My ancestors were fiery rocks that boomed
    from heaven. With me grim thunder lords drove
rain hard inside the seed. After a storm
    the smell of metal. I was pried from fields
and lashed to sticks and came of age with iron,
    armies crossing continents on horseback
and aftermaths of quiet.
                  Cool and heavy,
I work loud, but my element is silence.
The frame goes up, the roof laid on. Wires, pipes,
    shiny ductwork busy the interior.
Drywall and fixtures. I'm the force
    that broods through all the echoing rooms.

Sun Surveys Other Cynosures

> *I was all hot for honors, money, marriage, and You made mock of my hotness.*
> —St. Augustine, Confessions

A cosmopolitan stuck in the sticks,
far from the worst, and farther from the great,
I'm like the Sears of space—a middle-aged

star of medium brilliance near the edge
of a third-tier galaxy, constant solace
for this ragtag crew of sequins that cling

to my bright hem ("bright" *relatively*).
Alone = All One. So these dimwits
made me their Ra, Ra God, Sol, single-most

source of their metaphors—their girlfriend's eyes,
their hero's gold shield, their cloudy explosions.
Them – me = desolation.

From my semi-splendid isolation
I glare at inner-galaxy big shots glittering
among themselves, too grandiose to notice

me, singing solitary rounds of "O
sole mio" solely for my benefit.
Giant stars are too distant for my wit.

Moon at the Mirror

Location, location, location.
Even when I'm a slivered wafer
blanked out by the big guy, I got pull.

Just a shiny rock? So what. I'm close.
Others triumph in looks and power
but watch them fade as darkness brightens—

the big brassy moment I show up
(I adore being a blond), entrancing
homesick soldiers and drowning poets.

Thorn Gets Theoretical

You got it wrong. I'm no escort,
      a sword protecting a bit of fluff.
The flower was my idea. Sure,
      my only one, but one's enough.

There's nothing quite as gratifying
      as watching a bright face go slack
then crumple in pain. You're just dying
      to say it, go on: I'm a prick,

but you got to admit I'm clever
      posing as a mousy brown twig
when I can flash quick as a cleaver.
      There. You know you deserve that sting.

Though flowers open and break down,
      exposing their sexual wares
to the rough wind, I stick around
      exacting payment from the careless.

Despair's Rope of Sands

I am a straw that sucks the ocean up.
    Now look what I've done with my awful thirst

for attention. The seafloor's a stinking mat
    of worries, whelks, and weeds where smothered fish

flap like shingles—slippery stepping stones
    that make a sad roof for my grand ambitions.

See what my sighing has done? A short pier's
    a disappointed bridge and clouds are shiftless.

I can't bear it, the turtle lumbering out
    to dribble her eggs in a washed up shoe.

Potato Speculates on Popularity

I don't want trouble, but the rutabagas
and the turnips—especially the turnips—
are muttering Ingrate, Upstart, and throwing
me looks. Sheez, Louise. I'm hardly escarole.
So I got lots of friends? I'm adaptable,
a hard worker, and I don't ask favors.
Put them in a basket and they're bitter.
Put them in a pan, better be copper.
The butter's too pale, the pepper's too coarse.
On and on. With me if I'm forgotten,
I turn extra-spective and gregarious.
I'm not called the Dirt Apple for nothing.
I stick my necks out at any bright chink
and light out for the garden on leafy legs.

Talk Radio

Static stretches between towns and headlights
grope the shoulder gravel while frets of me
roar and fade around turns. I'm a cloud crossing
the county on my hair of rain. When I'm forgotten
and untuned, I'm the sound of water seized
into ice. By your bed I stare all night,

hoisting the scores to another contest
you lose. When I'm remembered, I'm the fire
a match speaks to gasoline. The winter
you were seventeen none of it was fair,
but what'd you expect? You can't
carry justice in a spoon like cough syrup.

Where I go, I go shuddering—hammer,
anvil, stirrup—but remain untouched.
Puddles, the shush of tires at 4 A.M.,
even the broken bootstrap in your hand
care more for you than I ever will. Now
stop your crying. You know I don't hear you.

"Envy Has No Holidays"

—Francis Bacon 1561–1626

Once the mirror mists over, moisture
beading on the faucets and along my nose,
and I lower myself to my chin
in hot water that laps the tub's rim,

makes my skin flare, and nests tiny pearls
in my hair, the door opens and here they come.
They don't bother to shuck their coats
or set down their purses. They step right in,

shoes and all. Water sloshes out and makes a run
for the door, and they squeeze around me,
soaking it up, passing around the sponge
as I scramble into the soap dish to hurl at them

my iridescent insults, my ammo of bubbles.

Dog's Ars Poetica

Though its whiskers take the air's temperature, and its gritty tongue
    tastes the marrow of pleasure,
though it's rightly proud of its skill in the stalk, how camouflaged as a
    collapsed staircase, it catapults at a twitching wing,
though all grace and cunning,
a cat is no good at poetry.
It spits at water and brings you only a dumb tangle of tendon.

No, it requires me. Slobbery and faithful,
strictly disciplined yet eager and modest,
I can enter a lake without a wrinkle
and what I bring back, secure in my black
mouth, is unbloodied—alive and terrified.

Lace Sings a Madrigal

My towns once were cities and my villages
    once were towns. A river takes a new turn
and leaves its slight cousin, a silver rill
    that rarely says a word. Silt fills a harbor.

The quiet basks. It stretches out and dreams
    of me, light scriptorium, galaxy
    in thread invisible as gravity.
Simple and twisted loops, I'm what it means

to love something into complexity,
my gauzy patience you call ecstasy.

Leaf's Lay of the Everlasting

"Márgarét, áre you gríeving . . . ?"

To you birth is detachment, clamp
    and cut, and a blackened stump
identifies you as one born
    from one, enthralled by borders,
accounting, and singularity.
    To me birth is fluid since
I have no edges. What you feel
    as precipice, to me
is open window. I'm the vowels
    rowing in the canal.
Sun sponge, full page, airy kitchen
    cooking air, I'm the lips
around the aria.
        But you know
me well when you let go
of your ledge, spilling buckets
    of ledgers from your head,
when you let go and come tumbling:
    slow leaves, a sunlit bed.

Bad News

And I'm caught in the bubble now, glass house
floating with me inside. My sister's voice
has sudden silver contours through the phone,
slopes, crags, a stream that seems to be
clattering over gravel. Not yet, the bubble says

because its disposition is to tease—
iridescence, surface tension, aloft.
This one will make the fence and keep on going.
And then this moment, which moments from now
will seem foreign and smooth, breaks into pieces

like a windshield, square tears of safety glass
raining down, a puddle of block type to set
the newspapers of the dead. No more passage.
His young doctor was wrong. There wasn't time
enough to see my father again.

Another Great Library Burns

"and his dying was the conflagration of a great library . . ."

Shouts and cries as engines labor
on pump ships in the harbor. Water
clanks against the flames in Archives
where murals curl and hiss. Its Laurentian
staircase quavers, grillwork fusing
and buckling, as the fire breaks out
and rushes at the crowd. We stumble back
over crates and hoses, against warehouses,
faces glowing as we grope for each other's sleeves.
Like reverse snow trembling on vague currents,
cinders drift into our hair and weep
from our eyes. A few manuscripts
on crackling parchment are hustled out,
an oil painting, some crumbling histories,
the stamp collection begun in 1938
with three stamps affixed at the clean
kitchen table, that apartment on Reading Road
where an all-night Hardee's now stands.
The tricky curtain of fire shimmies shelf to shelf,
a steady hunger that streams down gangplanks,
into corners, up spines. Leather, paper, ink
go in a gulp—the Union's blunders at Shiloh,
a speech from *A Midsummer Night's Dream*
(he was Oberon at Walnut Hills High),
Johnny Vander Meer's back-to-back no hitters,
a joke about God golfing with a priest, a poem

by Housman, and where to find a drink
Sunday morning. And what to me is the loss
of Aristotle's *Dialogues* or Aeschylus's
Prometheus, next to the sound
of my father's voice one more time?

Appeal

The evidence lies
in the shriveled woods,
the testimony
of walnuts thudding
the road, and the moon
gulped to an elbow
corroborates it:
everything must end,
perfectly natural.
But why accept it?
I'll be the steadfast
sea captain's daughter
waiting for some news
of the lost vessel,
patrolling the shore
with long sticks, stirring
flotsam and foam, oh,
the patter of hope
in a swollen shoe.
I want to leak sand
from my fists and lick
the grit from my lips,
become the loyal
lighthouse whose windows
burn a hundred years.

The evidence I
put my hand on, cool
hardened facts I bent

over and kissed and
kissed, his neck tie
blooming with my tears—
Patch me, I'm leaking—
I quipped to my stumped
sisters and brothers.
(How can you when he
hurt us all so much?)
That evidence was
only physical.
I was unconquered.
All these months, it's still
unsupportable,
too wrong to admit:
my father is dead.

Find the false bottom,
find the tampered proof,
that will be the way
he went, rattling trees,
scrambling where moonlight
can't catch him, hunkered
behind his bleary
eyeglasses, a slick
and manifold seed.

Don't

Along the furry case, the seams
ease open and the bud drops out.
Waxy petals uncurl in the moist
night air. The fresh face turns

to the banged-up moon climbing
again in its wreath of ancient
silence. Grief is a night bloomer
and when it opens up, it opens

to cup the dark and rock it
on its wet stem. Though moths come
and drink the juice, though creamy
perfumes ride the night, it remains

alone, remote, this white bruise,
beautiful and useless.

Steadily

> "You should have a softer pillow than my heart."
> —Byron, to his wife

In the sun-ladled spot we dug for it
the peach tree endeavors. It raises rain,
pumps it through hairy roots, trunk, branches, veins
and blows from itself like bubbles of spit

green fruits that are now blushing into peaches.
Why the rain forms a peach and not a plum
or walnut or star-ball of a sweetgum,
the tree can't say. It shivers in the breeze

with satisfaction, completely unfettered
by what it is or isn't. Sunshine cooks
in its leaves, leaves drop off, and the long dead
revive inside its arteries. These cricks

and drones and cryptic corridors—I'm tired
of sadness, the baroque rations of grief.
I have lived in thwarts and starts, a gray trial
of suspended time, since my father's death

while patient as rain you've waited for me
to draw you in and know you again bodily.

Luminous Blue Variables

If the stars should appear one night in a thousand years, how would men believe and adore; and preserve for many generations the remembrance of the city of God which had been shown! But every night come out these envoys of beauty, and light the universe with their admonishing smile.

—Emerson

Inside the hollow rock, following the sound
of water, still we climbed, he first and I second,
until I glimpsed through an opening

some of the beautiful cargo the sky carries.
And then I climbed out to see the stars again.
As I leaned back, taking long drinks of air

like someone draining a cold bucket,
my eyes opened farther and let the stars
behind the stars come forward. As the quiet

became a steady throb, I realized
he was gone. Though I looked for him feelingly
among the stiff shadows, starlit

rocks and bushes, I knew he had gone
at the moment of my deepest looking,
gone like a ship on the horizon,

a dimpling, an echo, then beyond

✦

the bronze gong of my father's voice

✦

If we could see far-red, infrared,
and ghostly ultraviolet, the ground would glow
with them, the sky would shower them.
While we stand on tiptoe looking out,

our eyes trained by common colors
borne by our sun, invisible powers
are riding the waves—are the waves—
gliding toward us, through us humming

as the killing glances shot by stars
darker and sharper roll off our foamy shield

✦

my father's voice sounded on the long waves
of radio, late into the night, rolling

✦

"Power is only Pain
Stranded, thro' Discipline"

✦

The bland afternoon, which seems a direct
plane of light, a window, misdirects me.
For indirection is the way
the world comes. The colors

of plants, sky, stones are spectral
signatures. We write our names in waves.
And the day's blue name blanks out the night.
But through the glare, through glass,

through sheetrock and shingles
the unseen envoys roll, fast and fretted—
silent whistle that makes the dog moan—
or long-sloped radio waves, postcards

mailed from the beginning of time.
We crouch at a slot in the door

✦

"Why, Mister, we get you better than some of those Atlanta stations"

✦

late into the night, top of the hour,
his voice tolled out the news—
holdup, police chase, river drowning—
rolled from nightstand, through car window
gliding under streetlights, rippled north
across cornfields, into Michigan and Canada,
and south, broadcast to truckers
bouncing on I-75, to Florida by morning
with static and starlight dimmed

✦

"This nine-pound meteorite crashed through the roof of a home occupied by Mrs. E. Hulitt Hodges in Sylacauga, Ala. at 1:00 P.M. C.S.T. on Nov. 30, 1954. It bounced off a console radio in her living room and hit her hip, which was bruised enough to require hospitalization."

◆

And as he came near that city
a sudden light glowed around him,
a light leaping from the sky,
and as he dropped to the ground
Saul heard a voice saying

◆

static and starlight dimmed
above the parked car where the radio
was tuned to the final innings
of the game we'd skipped,
I drew squiggles on the window, bored
with the boy and making out,
and at the top of the hour, I turned the volume up—
arson fire in Avondale, a shooting in Covington—
disasters to daunt my date from the suburbs,
rolling through us in the dark
on the disciplined voice of an errant man,
that easy beauty of my father's baritone

◆

"A light will suddenly appear. It quickly grows intensely bright, but it hardly seems to move. That is because it is headed right for the witness."

◆

She leans back inside the rain of gold,
bending and dipping so it splashes
against her skin. Looking up Danaea sees
she has become a tower of light that reaches
as far up as the sun reaches down.

When mortals are struck by the more-
than-mortal, an echo bounces back and back

◆

the easy beauty of his baritone fading,
he was happiest with a pack of cash
and a piano bar when someone asked him to sing,
crooner with a drink and a bad line
of credit, in his wallet a shrunken xerox
of his daughter's poem, sad poem
about him gone dim and dwindling,
and over the orbit of the glass—
where a planet bobbed on a toothpick axis—
he struck the bronze gong of his baritone

◆

"But, after all, death runs in that family."

◆

Forgive me I have called all you stars
false names—china chips, nailheads, punctures,

blue jean rivets, glitter—I was afraid
your grandeur would diminish me. And you

blue stars, luminous blue variables
who live hot and die quickest,

you show me when the greatest collapse,
it is as if one man and all his mock gravity

had been compressed into a single cell's
smallest locket where it throbs,

rolling out invisible messages.
Only when I was looking up,

the sky opening at my looking,
did I feel him gone and wholly unhurt.

One life is so small its story fits everywhere,
and even when the life comes to disaster,

the waves climb and crest and climb.
History is daylight, night eternity.

These Envoys

Billet-doux
bulletin
bright bullet

shooting toward
our cloud-hugged
planet (light

cable sent
from the far
dark) slides through

stratosphere
troposphere
city haze

reaching me
who looks up
from the cold

newspaper
I've picked up
5 A.M.

and my eyes
open wide
their veined gates

as the quick
message mounts
stairs, enters

the bower
that funnels
cascading

light into
this feeling
now I hear

you loud love

Flood Plain

      The land lies flooded and fat. The sun
jumped from the earth when the plane took off
      and now flashes from soggy fields—

someone behind a fence toting a lantern—
      now it flares out in a pond, now a river,
now a slow, steady looking from a lake,

      then it plunges away from me
until the next flooded furrows.
      How was I ever gloomy? How did I

let myself forget this quickening?
      Flickering fields, luscious umber mud,
already a few trees decked in that aching

      green of early spring. Gray and dutiful,
the plane drones around me. Far below
      its shadow skims and bends over barns,

brave solitary farmhouses, highways
      and nervy cars. How can it be
that we die? How is it that we can shush and set

      our faces toward the north, the shades
drawn down after us, while all about us
      is fluent and flashing and vast?

Notes

"Done": In memory of my father-in-law, Dominik Stroik, 1918–1993.

"At My Brother's Place": Two years later he said, "I know there is flesh and I know there is spirit, but I don't know why it is me who sees spirit."

"Parchment": Thanks to Linda Voigts whose medieval manuscripts and expertise nurtured this poem.

"Two Winter Pictures": Jean, Duc de Berry, was son, brother, and uncle to kings of France and one of the richest men of his age, a fantastic connoisseur, collector of books, jewels, art, and exotic animals. We know relatively little about the Limbourg Brothers, the miniaturists who between 1413 and 1416 illuminated the *Très Riches Heures of Jean, Duc de Berry*, one of the masterpieces of the late Middle Ages. The Limbourgs were artisans, from the (always) rising middle class, but they apparently had a close enough relationship with the duke to present him with an elaborately made fake book for a New Year's present, described in the Duke's inventory as a *"livre contrefait d'une pièce de bois en semblance d'un livre, où il n'a nuls feuillets ne rien escript"* (book made from a piece of wood to resemble a book, with no pages and nothing written in it), a book, perhaps, that might be prized by someone thought to prefer luxuries to reading.

"Haloes Stippled with Crosses, Roses, Stars and Spears": Many of the details concerning slavery come from Hugh Thomas's, *The Slave Trade*.

"Relief from Nineveh": The last line is from *The Epic of Gilgamish*, VII, 38, N. K. Sanders, trans.

"Choir of Dust": For Martie Zelt, in memory of our friend Loretta Abston, 1933–1997.

"Chronicle of Hammer": E. C. Krupp in his *Beyond the Blue Horizon* describes the connections ancient peoples made between meteorites, hammers, and iron.

"Despair's Rope of Sands": "rope of sands," George Herbert, "The Collar"; "pier . . . disappointed bridge," Julian Barnes, *Flaubert's Parrot*.

"Leaf's Lay of the Everlasting": Epigraph, Hopkins, "Spring and Fall."

"Another Great Library Burns": "and his dying was the conflagration . . . ," Seymore Tekla, *Sevrin*; thanks to Lois Spatz for information about the holdings of the ancient library at Alexandria.

"Luminous Blue Variables": Epigraph, "Nature"; lines 2–4, Dante, *Inferno*, final three lines; "If we could see far-red . . . ," adapted from Bob Berman, *Secrets of the Night Sky;* "Power is only Pain . . . ," Dickinson, "The Bible is an antique Volume"; "Why, Mister . . . ," Lillian Carter to my father, 1976, except she said, "Why, Pat . . . ," (my father was a newscaster for WLW Radio in Cincinnati; its fifty-kilowatt broadcast easily heard in Plains, Georgia); "This nine-pound meteorite . . . ," photo caption, Krupp, above, "Hammer"; "Saul heard a voice saying," adapted from Acts:9:3; "A light will suddenly appear," Krupp, above. "But, after all, death runs . . . ," Elizabeth Bowen, *Death of the Heart*.